TRUMP IS NUTS!

An Illustrated Guide and Coloring Book on the Many Ways that Trump Has Gone Nuts

by Gini Graham Scott

Illustrations by Nick Alexander

TRUMP IS NUTS!

TABLE OF CONTENTS

INTRODUCTION

This book was inspired by the many discussions on Facebook and other social media sites by people who are appalled by Trump's rants and insults. Some created or shared cartoons that depicted Trump raging, and others shared or created names for Trump, such as Trumpelthinskin, Trump the Demented, Dingleberry Trump, Trumpty Dumpty, and more.

Many commenters even speculated that Trump was not merely a narcissist or sociopath, interested in only me, Me, ME!!!, humiliating anyone who opposed him, and winning whatever that took. But they also thought he was crazy, insane, and even suffering from early stage Alzheimer's.

Certainly, Trump's raging behavior and wild insults suggest a person who is out of control, unhinged, and literally nuts! And these ideas got me thinking about the many ways in which Trump might be nuts, using actual nuts to illustrate.

So in this spirit of wild and wacky fun, *Trump Is Nuts!* features a variety of nuts, along with nut cases and nuthouses, showing all the ways in which TRUMP might be considered NUTS! You might even grab some nuts and munch away, as you read this book and see Trump as many types of nuts.

A WHOLE LOT OF NUTS

When you get mixed nuts, you can't be sure of what you are getting, just that they will be mixed up. Likewise, the nuts who have joined with Trump are certainly a very mixed up lot, though they aren't very diverse. In fact, a lot of the nuts don't want to be mixed with others at all. They'd prefer to be in their own separate jar and hope others will want to buy that.

Mixed Nuts

Is Trump really a nut case? That's what more and more people believe, including some psychologists who have described him as having a "narcissistic personality disorder," whereby one thinks that everything is about me, me, me. Someone with this disorder also has delusions of grandeur about who one is and what one can do.   Such a person can never be wrong and is ready to attack anyone who stands in his way, disagrees, or criticizes him. He always has to win whatever he does and makes excuses should he lose at anything, so he still comes out on top.

In other words, if you're not with Trump, you're against him and are fair game for insults, threats, and whatever else Trump can come up with to demean and humiliate you, whether in the media or in court. As such, he shares traits with other larger-than-life leaders like Hitler and Mussolini, to whom he is often compared, and some consider them nutcases, too.

It's a Nut Case

Being considered nuts can be difficult, because people want to group you with a lot of sick and crazy people who need to be put away or often get sacked from a job, because they seem to be out of control. Sacking them is a little like bagging wild animals – the rangers just have to catch them before they harm other animals or escape from their natural habitat to harm others. Likewise, a growing number of people, including Republicans, think that Trump is going insane and pulling them into a deep dark hole with him. So you might say they need to bag him or sack him by saying "You're fired," which is one of Trump's favorite lines, though when it refers to someone else.

A Bag of Nuts

POWER NUTS

As they say, cash is king, and so are cashew nuts. At least, if you've got the cash or caché, anyone can be king, or at least act like one. But once people lose their cash or caché, they're out of luck and just another nut. After all, once their royal accoutrements, such as a fancy robe, scepter, and crown are gone, people have little to set them apart from all the other mixed and mixed up nuts out there in the world, and they can easily get squashed.

In short, if you take the cash away from a cashew, what do you have left – just a great big EW!

Trumpking Cashew Nut

Almonds are everywhere – in cakes, cookies, and ice cream toppings. There is even an Almond Joy candy bar.   But the Trump Almond Power Bar is in a class by itself, because it packs so much power. It'll give you more energy, assurance, and strength, so you can readily knock down, insult, and humiliate anyone you want – just like Trump does!

Trump Almond Power Bar

The Macadamia Nut is a round, hard shelled nut, which came to the U.S. from Australia by way of Hawaii. So it might be considered like a tough military nut, known for its strength and prowess – a tough nut to crack.

Yet, because it comes from elsewhere, it's not true blue American. So as an immigrant nut, maybe it should be deported, and never allowed to return to these shores, much less the supermarket shelves of America. As they say in the Marines – "Semper Fi!" And as they now say of this nut: "Bye, bye, Macadamia, goodbye."

Macadamia Nut (aka Military Nut)

The Trumpflower Seed is like a lowly Sunflower Seed, which became even tougher. So you might think of it like a warrior which attacks anything that might try to eat it up, such as birds flying by. In the process, it might even take down the American Eagle and all it represents – from the democratic courts to the laws of the land. The Trumpflower just has to spread enough of its seeds throughout the countryside, and soon there will be Trumpflowers everywhere. Thus, as the Trumpflower grows up big and strong, it will cover the land, so any plants that get in its way will soon wither and die. It all starts with a single seed that grows wild and crazy and out of control.

Trumpflower Seed

The Hickory Nut is definitely a super-powerful hard nut to crack. It is known for its hard, tough, nearly unbreakable shell, and the hickory tree with its often shaggy bark was perfect for making hickory sticks and switches, used to strike fear into anyone in danger of being hit. No wonder, at times, it became the rod of choice by jailers and schoolteachers for punishing anyone, when such punishments were legal.

If you've heard the expression, "spare the rod and spoil the child," most likely a hickory stick inspired those words of advice. Another popular expression, "Sticks and stones might break my bones," might be inspired by a hickory stick beating, too.

Now Trump would seem to be a great advocate for using this stick along with other methods of torture, including waterboarding, to bring any miscreants – or anyone who disagrees with him – to heel, and later to "heal." So as you can see, he's like a judge ready to dole out justice, which could be a good beating with a hickory stick from a hickory tree full of hickory nuts that could even double as stones should you want to stone anyone.

Hickory Nuts

TOUGH NUTS

The Wall-Nut, also popularly known as a Walnut, is great for creating walls, as well as in building all kinds of furniture, since it has a very strong, hard exterior that covers up its soft interior. Perhaps it's so strong on the outside to protect its inner insecurity. In fact, this inner nut is composed of two sections which look very much like the lobes of a human brain, where the left side is all about being rational, and the right side is all about being intuitive and emotional. If they are in balance, great. Otherwise – well, things can go boom in the night – or in the day, too. But the Wall-Nut can help, because it has long been used in gunstocks, as well as in cabinetwork. Plus the wall can be like the wall of a castle – keeping anyone and everyone out, while shooting now and asking questions later.

Wall-Nut

This pecan is a nut with old Southern roots, so no wonder it's proud of its old Southern traditions, from delicious pecan pies to KKK hoods, which are shaped much like the end of a pecan. Just poke in two holes and paint the pecan nut white, and voila, you've got a hood. In fact, since the pecan has a smooth, thin shell, it's perfect for heating up to make a pecan pie. But you don't want to stir it up too much, because then, due to its thin skin, it could easily explode and make a great big mess – in the kitchen or anywhere else, just like the KKK is making a big mess of things in the U.S. today.

Southern Pecan

Though the Cashew Nut is known for being one of the most popular nuts around, it is not really a real nut. Instead, it is a strange kidney-shaped seed that grows outside the bottom of a hanging fruit. Moreover, the cashew is only edible when roasted, so it is actually toxic at other times. In other words, it is a fraudulent nut that is called a nut because of its outer appearance. But then it could be very painful and difficult to impossible to digest, if it's not handled the right way. Even so, it might still claim to be a real nut, and others might claim this, too -- much like Trump and his followers often don't know what's true or real, and don't care.

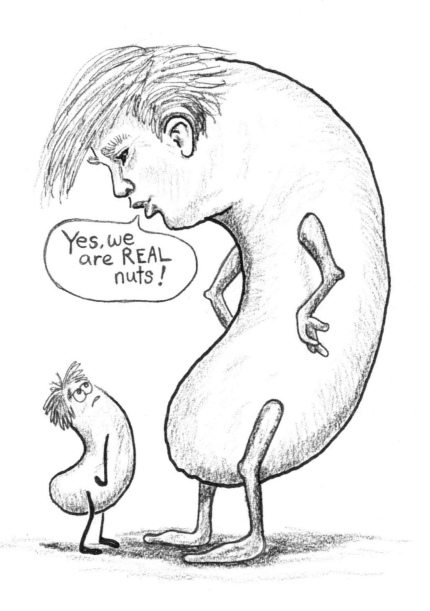

Just a Regular Cashew Nut

The Trumpkin Seed is one tough cookie…er seed, since it's not really a nut. Rather, it's a very strong seed, which comes from the pumpkin, a large, pulpy round fruit with a thick, orange-yellow rind that looks very much like Trump, who is sometimes called the Orange Man. Then again, with a few deep knife cuts, you have carved out the eyes, nose, and mouth to make a perfect Trump-O-Lantern for Halloween. Just have to put it in the window, and you can variously welcome or scare the neighbors, depending on whether you want to let them in or keep them out.

Still another characteristic of the Trumpkin Seed is that it's one of nature's testosterone boosters, which can quickly pump you up, so you can do well in a fight. Just pick out your enemies and start attacking them, thinking that testosterone boost will help you win. But all that testosterone can often make you testy, so if you pick the wrong fight with the wrong opponent, you might easily lose. Then in the end, they may say you've gone to seed, because you really weren't a tough nut after all.

Trumpkin Seed

MONEY NUTS

The Hazeltrump Nut, which comes from a variety of small shrubs or trees and has a smooth brown shell, has great bona fides as a native of North America and Europe, which is most known for its creamy spread. So it has been packaged as a great spread that you can put over anything. Or maybe use it to put over anything on anyone. It's especially good on bread – or for making bread through branding.

In fact, it's such a good spread, that you can put it in a jar and spread it everywhere and anywhere, which makes it an ideal surface spread. But look under the surface or try to get rid of it, and it can look a little like…well, you know, especially when you put globs of it together. Then, it can turn into a pile of…well, a Hazeltrump Nut paste, what did you think?

Hazeltrump Nut

Have you heard of a wingnut? Well, you will soon, because it will have the Trump Wingnut brand on it, just like Trump has branded steaks, vodka, casinos, health products, and a university. What's next? Why not wingnuts, since no one has thought to put a brand name on them. They are just put in a section of a shelf with all the other nuts, bolts, screws, and other hardware items. But now, with the Trump brand on wingnuts, hardware stores can announce these nuts are special and charge two or three times as much. The result is more money for everyone, unless of course, people decide to skip the Trump Wingnuts to get regular nuts, which are the same, but cost much less.

What's next if the wingnuts idea gets clipped? Maybe Trump screws. And why not? Trump is the expert in screwing up and screwing everyone.

Trump Wingnut Special

VERY NUTTY NUTS

Consider the Trump Coconut. Just like any coconut, it's got a hard shell outside, with lots of fuzzy barbs, so it looks like a head covered with frizzy hair. It's all white inside, like all good coconuts. Unfortunately, when coconuts fall out of trees in a tropical paradise, where many grow, they can crack open. That's how many coconuts get cracked, and when that happens, an army of ants can eat them up, just like an army of protesters can appear at the big Trump rallies and events. However, when attacked, uncracked coconuts can make great cannonballs to fire back – which is a good way to keep all that good white coconut meat inside.

The Trump Coconut

As its name suggests, the Brazil Nut hails from tropical South America, where it comes from a tree that bears hard, round, wood pods with about 20 to 30 nuts each. You might say this is like a community of nuts, where a group of nuts surround and protect all of the other nuts. However, if you get one nut alone, that could be very scary for it, because it could easily be eaten up. But before it is, it will fight like hell, and yell and scream to get away. But maybe it can't, and then it's goodbye Brazil. Still, you better not monkey around with this nut, because it's prone to throwing fits.

Brazil Trumpnut

Consider the Trump Pistachio Nut, which comes from the Mediterranean region and Western Asia, but mostly it's known for having an oily green kernel under its small hard shell. If you've ever had pistachio ice cream, you know it's unique for being very green. Well, that's just like Trump – very green because he is so new at trying to run for anything – from running for office to running the country, and being green, he doesn't know what he doesn't know.

Today, being green has become very popular, but there are all kinds of green, from greens on the golf course to the lush green of elegant lawns and having plenty of greenbacks or cash. And Trump is all of those, so the Trump Pistachio Nut fits him to a T for Trump – and it makes a great tea, too, which could be packaged and sold as one more Trump brand to buy and buy.

Pistachio Trumpnut

Sometimes people who act crazy are called "nutty as a fruitcake." They might also be called nutty as a "nutmeg," because this spice not only adds a spicy flavor in cooking, but in higher doses, it is used as an aphrodisiac and for its psychoactive effects. And the excessive use of nutmeg is definitely not recommended for people with psychiatric conditions, because it can make them go super nuts.

For example, if psychiatrists think someone has a narcissistic personality disorder, is a sociopath, or has delusions of grandeur or megalomania, they would not give that person any nutmeg. If they did, the person could go really cuckoo and tell their followers all kinds of crazy things about what they can do to get people to follow them. As a result, the nuts on nutmeg can have a very powerful effect with their mad ravings at big rallies, where their followers might think they are really GREAT rather than just GRATING. In fact, the Nutty Nutmeggers could even think they could shoot someone on a main street and their followers would still follow them – maybe even over a cliff. They just have to say whatever they want, and their followers will follow.

Nutty Nutmeg

A nuthouse is a perfect place for nuts, so as an alternative to the White House, some think that's a more suitable place for nut cases that are truly nuts. But it's up to the electorate to decide – though sometimes people who could belong in the nuthouse might end up in the White House and vice versa, since there's no qualifying nut test to determine if someone is certified to be President, such as being born in the United States. On the other hand, if one is properly certified, one can end up in the nuthouse. Or is the system nuts, because it isn't always possible to tell who's really nutty, and some of our policies are really nuts?

Welcome to the Nut House

NO MORE NUTS

As they say, from little acorns, big oaks grow. But that's only some of the time from this thick-walled nut that's usually set in a woody, cuplike base. Unfortunately, sometimes, mighty oaks can get off to a very bad start, such as if they get stepped on by a passing hiker or eaten up by a squirrel. Then, too, as the climate gets warmer and warmer, though some try to deny there is any climate change, a budding oak tree can shrivel up and die, because it is too hot and dry. It could even be consumed by a fire from lightning or a passing war. And sometimes small white worms can worm their way into these acorns. So instead of the beginnings of a strong, sturdy oak, out pops a small wiggly worm. Though you never know – Will it be an oak? Will it be a worm? Or will the acorn get squashed – so it will never become a mighty oak.

Fallen Acorn

Getting down to the nuts and bolts is like getting down to the brass tacks of something. Either way, you've got to know what you are doing, or you could end up with a screw loose. Or you might get a screwy idea, like a bolt from the blue, and then you could get really screwed. Thus, if Trump sometimes – or increasingly – seems to be losing it, perhaps that's why, which is why more and more people – from Democrats and independents to former Trumpkins, hope he mightt bolt away, like a horse bolting from a barn. However, in this case, no one regrets leaving the barn door open – they just hope the horse will run very far away and never come back. Usually people throw away the shells and enjoy the nut, but in this case, a growing number of people just want to throw away the nut.

Getting Down to the Nuts and Bolts

ABOUT THE AUTHOR AND ILLUSTRATOR

Gini Graham Scott - Author

Gini Graham Scott has published over 50 books with mainstream publishers, focusing on social trends, work and business relationships, and personal and professional development. Some of these books include *Scammed* and *Lies and Liars: How and Why Sociopaths Lie and How to Detect and Deal With Them.*

She has written a series of unique commentaries on the 2016 election which include *2016 Election Fairy Tales, 2016 Election Monsters, Myths, and Mayhem, The Battles of Donnie and Teddy: 4 Children's Stories About the 2016 Election for Adults*, and *Trump Is Nuts!*

She has gained extensive media interest for previous books, including appearances on *Good Morning America, Oprah, Montel Williams, CNN,* and hundreds of radio shows. She is often quoted by the media and has websites at www.ginigrahamscott.com and www.changemakerspublishingandwriting.com. She has about 45,000 listings in Google Search Results.

She has been a regular Huffington Post blogger since December 2012 and has a Facebook page at www.facebook.com/changemakerspublishing. These stories about the election first appeared as Huffington Post blogs.

She has written, produced, and sometimes directed over 60 short videos, which are featured on her Changemakers Productions website at www.changemakersproductions.com and on YouTube at www.youtube.com/changemakersprod.

Her screenplays, mostly in the drama, crime, legal thriller, and sci-fi genres, include several dealing with changes in science, technology, business, and society, including *The New Child, New Identity,* and *Dead No More.* These are in development with trailers, business plans, and interested directors and talent.

Her feature, *Suicide Party #Save Dave*, which she wrote and executive produced, will be released by RSquared Films, in the summer 2016. Details are at www.suicidepartyfilm.com. Her second feature *Driver* has just been filmed and will be released in 2017. More details are at www.facebook.com/driverthefilm.

She has a PhD in sociology from U.C. Berkeley and MAs in anthropology, pop culture and lifestyles, recreation and tourism, and mass communications and organizational/consumer/audience behavior from Cal State, East Bay. She is getting an MA in communications there in 2017.

Nick Alexander - Illustrator

Writer/artist Nick Alexander was born and raised in New Jersey in a boating family. His first short story was published at the age of 14 in a national magazine. He has since written stage and screenplays some of which have won awards and been produced and numerous short stories. His traditionally published novels include historical fiction, fantasy. and science fiction. His illustrations have appeared in various publications from children's picture books to political cartoons in newspapers and online. He presently resides outside Sedona, Arizona.

CHANGEMAKERS PUBLISHING
3527 Mt. Diablo Blvd., #273
Lafayette, CA 94549
www.changemakerspublishing.com
(925) 385-0608 . changemakers@pacbell.net

CPSIA information can be obtained
at www.ICGtesting.com
Printed in the USA
BVHW010601290420
578809BV00009B/40